# The GJB Guide
## Crocheted Dolls

Nikki Olida

The GJB Guide: Crocheted Dolls
Copyright © 2013 by Nikki Olida

Publisher: CreateSpace
Editors: Myro Joy Lee & Kevin Cheng
Design and Layout: Nikki Olida
Illustrations: Nikki Olida
Photography: Myro Joy Lee & Nikki Olida

"YouTube" is a registered trademark of Google, Inc. "Google" is a registered trademark of Google, Inc. "Etsy" is a trademark of Etsy, Inc. "Facebook" is a registered trademark of Facebook, Inc. "Red Heart" is a registered trademark of J. & P. Coats. "JOANN.COM" is a registered trademark of Jo-Ann Stores, Inc. "Susan Bates" is a registered trademark of Susan Bates, Inc., C. J. Bates & Son. "Clover Takumi" is a registered trademark of Clover Needlecraft, Inc. "Boye" is a registered trademark of Wm. Wright Co. "Mettler" is a registered trademark of Mettler Threads. "Poly-Fil" is a registered trademark of J. & P. Coats. "Michaels" is a registered trademark of Michaels Stores, Inc. "Gingher" is a registered trademark of Gingher Corporation. "PlayStation" is a registered trademark of Sony Computer Entertainment Inc. "CNET" is a registered trademark of CBS Interactive Inc. "KOTAKU" is a trademark of Blogwire Hungary Szellemi Lemi Alkotast Hasznosito Kft.

ISBN-13: 9781493573578
ISBN-10: 1493573578

Printed in the U.S.A.

Mission Statement:
To spread the art of crocheting dolls around the globe.

This is dedicated to my family and all my fans

Creativity is in all of us.
You just have to look in the right places
and when you find it,
hold on to it with all your might.

# Preface

I am not quite sure how I began to be interested in crocheting but, once I started, I was hooked. Ever since I was little, I was drawn to art. That was my favorite class to go to when I was in school, aside from Math. I remember my mother teaching my sister and me how to crochet and knit. The first things I made were scarves and hats. When I attended college I stopped making things and took a long break. I started drawing for a short time and then got back into crocheting. Many have asked me what got me started in making video game dolls. I cannot pinpoint exactly but I remember seeing a stuffed Sackboy doll and wanting to make one for myself. I began making Totoros from the anime, "My Neighbor Totoro" and after that I made my very first Sackboy. This was when my YouTube "career" started. I started getting messages and comments on how to make one. Viewers wanted to know how they could make one of their own.

Now that I have been on YouTube for three years, I have thought about selling my patterns. I have sold several on Etsy and now I have produced this book as a more comprehensive guide. This is my first book so please message me on my Facebook for any suggestions you might have for my next one. For those who have purchased this book, I thank you :)!

# Introduction

This book is meant for beginner doll-makers with some basic knowledge of crocheting and a little sewing/needlework. Some of the content, althought referring to beginner/basic techniques, have stemmed from audience questions and thus have been included in the manuscript. Otherwise, if you need any other help with beginner techniques not described here, it would be best to watch some YouTube tutorials or read some explanations beforehand to supplement your understanding before you begin work on a doll. I have several introductory videos on my YouTube channel and these videos are listed in Appendix B.

I hope this book inspires you to make wonderful dolls that you or your friends and family can enjoy.

# Acknowledgements

There are many people I want to thank for helping me create this book. First of all, I want to thank my mother for teaching my sister and me how to crochet. It all started all those years ago. If it was not for my mother, I would not have discovered my love of crocheting. I would also like to thank those of you who have contributed in making this book possible. Without your generosity and support, this book would have just been an idea and nothing more. I would like to thank the following people:

Mena Soliman

Olivia Mawi

Marcia Scarpelli

Helmut Padilla

Kirrell

Rebecca Ramsey

Michael "Bulldozer" Frank

Nicola Fraser

Jason Epstein

John

Maiju

Sarah Burrough

Tsukeeno's

Aundrea Munson

Sarah Viall

Jennifer Leising

Rosie C.

Ronnie Johnson

Diem Tran

Shelina

Noemi Freixas

Stephanie Starling

Julianne Winter

Vickie F.

TTM

Steve M. Fletcher

Connie Taylor

Brit Alexander

Amanda Pizarro

Christine Sullivan

Shael Hawman

Dawn Klein

Phoxnake

Ashley Gygax

Fernando Perez

Jonelle Schulz

Kelly Ziemski

Andrenna Caballero

Kim Hayhurst

FluffsFluffy

ARP

Kat Kruse

Mitxuko

Jennifer Wang

Stephanie Viesca

Galapatron Stephanie

Alicia W.

Sandy Lam

Christie Fang

Jenneida

Mary Vu

Charlotte Anne Churchill

Amanda Gonzalez

Anthony Liang

Carolina Lannes

The Radford Family

# Acknowledgements

Sondra Yee

Michael D Lee

Sammy

Grace Huynh

Roesyenny Arifin

Westley Wong

Pamela Mercedes-Morris

Pam Jacques

Ken Cheng

Joy Jakubaitis

Barbara Jones

Sewen

San San Chan

Josh Gilbert

Sarah Hopes

Dinky Dana

Littledib

Eva Folgar

Jeannine Verburgt

Cassy Cane

Daisy Hernandez

Jessica Maus

Barbara Ortiz

# Table Of Contents

# Make Your Very Own Dolls

# Supplies

There are many brands of yarn from which to choose. You may feel over-whelmed when you first walk into a craft store or a local yarn store. I know I was! Choosing the type of yarn mostly depends on what type of texture you would like for your finished product. The softer yarns are going to be more expensive and the rougher ones are typically cheaper. The rougher yarns feel sturdier and I tend to choose those types over softer ones. I usually purchase Red Heart worsted weight yarn because it is the cheapest and they have so many colors to choose from. One thing you have to watch for is that different colors vary in thickness even within the same brand. Sometimes the darker colored yarns, like black, feel thick-er. With this in mind, the pattern would change slightly depending on the color you are using. So if you would like to change the color of a particular pattern you are using, it might not be the same size as the original project.

Buttons are what brings life to my dolls. The shinier, the better. Dull but-tons make the dolls look lifeless and a little creepy at times. When I started making dolls, I used buttons I purchased from Jo-Ann Fabrics. They were the perfect size for the Sackboys I was making. However, the store's supply of these buttons slowly depleted and I could no longer find them. I went online to see if I could find them and I did. After a while, I could not find them online either, so I moved on to a different kind of button. The buttons I would look out for are smooth, rounded and plain (see cover, p. 2, 28, 36 for dolls using these buttons). They are plastic and do not have holes in them. I found several buttons like this on Etsy. Some-times they would be out of stock, but Etsy is the only place I can find them nowadays. When you find them, stock up, because you never know when you are going to find them again. Just search for "shank buttons" on Etsy and you will find them. There are also buttons called "safety eyes". These can also be used and can be found on Etsy.

As with any doll project, you will need needles and thread. The darning needle I use is metal but there are also plastic ones out there. I would rec-ommend getting the metal ones because they are sturdier. I used plastic ones in the past but they tend to break. The Clover brand of darning needles is one I have used. The needle even comes with a plastic case. For sewing purposes, I use a sewing needle and thread. The thread I am using

# Supplies

presently is Mettler Metrosene Cordonnet. This thread is more durable for making dolls.

What is a doll without the stuffing? It is what makes your doll soft and cuddly. I do not have any preference when it comes to stuffing but I usually purchase the Fairfield Poly-Fil stuffing at Jo-Ann Fabrics or Michaels. Get the 20 oz. bag because even though you think you will just need a little bit of stuffing, you will end up using a lot of it. It is also helpful to have a small pair of scissors handy. I use the Gingher brand scissors that come with a cover. These types of scissors are portable and the cover prevents you from poking yourself or the container it is in. Row counters are optional. An alternative to row counters is using scrap yarn to keep track of the rows you have.

# Making The Basic Doll

A doll typically begins with a circular shape. Crocheting, in my opinion, is the easier method to make dolls. It is very flexible and you can make pretty much any shape that you want. Once you get the hang of making a basic doll, you can add accessories and even modify the pattern around to your liking.

This book will start with basic skills that will culminate in a basic doll, Benjamin. From here, you can create accessories and even change the colors. This doll is based on the Sackboys I make on my YouTube channel. Benjamin is simpler than a Sackboy because he does not have a zipper and only has three fingers on each hand. This is just one variation among the many you can make. This book will include techniques I have used to make it easier and decrease the amount of sewing you do. Sewing limbs on dolls and trying to figure out if they are symmetric are tedious tasks that can be eliminated. I like to sew as little as possible.

Little by little, I have shown you how to make dolls on my YouTube page. This book will simplify doll making and before you know it, you will be making and designing your own dolls.

# Making Your Circle

The majority of dolls you will be making will start with a circle. The regular circle begins with 2 chains and you would create your circle in the second chain from your crochet hook. The alternative "cleaner-looking" circle is the "magic circle". This circle starts with a loop and does not leave a hole in the middle of the circle. I prefer the magic circle because you do not have to worry about leaving a gap in the middle. Both of these circles are harder to explain in a book but these methods are shown on my YouTube page. Links to these are in Appendix B.

When making a circle larger, you will notice that it starts to take on a shape of a polygon with distinct corners. This is shown in Figure 1. This is normal because whenever you do 2 single crochets in one stitch you create a point. Doing this repeatedly in the same area will make that particular area have a corner.

Figure 1. Increasing the circle.

When crocheting, pay attention to what 1 single crochet (sc) looks like compared to 2 sc created in 1 stitch. This is helpful when you lose your place and you are trying to figure out what to do next. Figure 2, on the next page shows what this looks like. Once you learn to recognize this, you will not have to unravel everything and start over for that row. It saves a lot of time.

# Making Your Circle

Figure 2.

The yellow highlighted stitches (where more than 2 lines are highlighted) show what 2 single crochets in a stitch look like. The blue highlighted stitch (where only 2 lines are highlighted) show what 1 single crochet in a stitch looks like.

# Keeping Track Of Rows

You can get a row counter to keep track of your rows but you can also use yarn. After each row you can insert yarn through the last stitch you made. Use a different colored yarn so you can tell the difference between the marker and what you are making. In Figure 3 shows what this looks like. This makes it easy to count how many rows you have already finished. When using really dark colored yarn, try not to use white or cream yarn as a marker because several fibers can be left on your work and it can be a bit annoying to try and pick them off. The same goes for light colored yarn and dark yarn for markers.

Figure 3. Using scrap yarn as a marker.

# Dissecting Patterns

Making a pattern for a doll is easy once you know how to manipulate a simple pattern. The first step is usually creating the circle and the next steps involve increasing by adding stitches evenly in each row. Step 2 is where you start increasing by creating 2 single crochets in each stitch for that row. From here, the steps follow a sequential pattern. Take a look at the pattern below.

6sc in magic circle. [6]
2sc in each st around. [12]
(1sc in first st. 2sc in next st.) X 6 [18]
(1sc in first 2 st. 2sc in next st.) X 6 [24]
(1sc in first 3 st. 2sc in next st.) X 6 [30]
(1sc in first 4 st. 2sc in next st.) X 6 [36]

You start to see a "pattern" forming in the pattern. Certain numbers in the pattern are increasing in a predictable manner. Let us briefly look at how increasing works. Think of each of these steps as having 3 separate variables in which one does not change. Here you can see the pattern in terms of variables:(1sc in X st. 2sc in next st.) X Y [Z]. "X" and "Z" are the ones that change and "Y" is constant. In other patterns , "Y" might change, but for simple doll patterns, "Y" does not change.

1. 6sc in magic circle.
2. 2sc in each st around. [12]
3. (1sc in first st.  2sc in next st.)  X 6    [18]

In many patterns, the first highlighted area is the part that changes when you increase. So it might be easier to see this part of the pattern as: "1sc in Xst," where "X" is the variable that changes. The pattern, depending on how large you want the doll, can be written like this:

(1sc in first st. 2sc in next st.) X 6 [18]
(1sc in first 2 st. 2sc in next st.) X 6 [24]
(1sc in first 3 st. 2sc in next st.) X 6 [30]
etcetera...

9

# Dissecting Patterns

You can see here that "X" equals "first, first 2, first 3...etc."

In the second highlighted area, this part usually stays constant if you want to gradually increase and make your circle larger. Let us assign this a variable called "Y".

In the last highlighted area, this increases as you add more stitches. Let us call this variable, "Z." So in this pattern, when you repeat step 3 six times, you have added 6 stitches to the row. So you are going to want to add 6 to Y (which in the previous row was 12; adding 6 to 12 will give you 18).

# Creating Corners

To create an edge, crocheting only in one loop can do the trick. Figure 4 shows which ones are the back loops and which ones are front loops. Figure 5 shows the "line" that forms after crocheting in all the back loops.

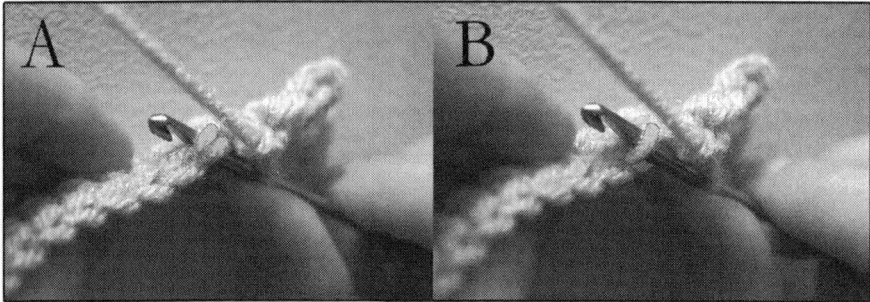

Figure 4A. In both loops. Figure 4B. Only in back loop.

Stitches are typically made up of two loops. For a regular stitch you would put your crochet hook through both loops as shown in Figure 4A. Figure 4B shows the crochet hook going into the back loop only.

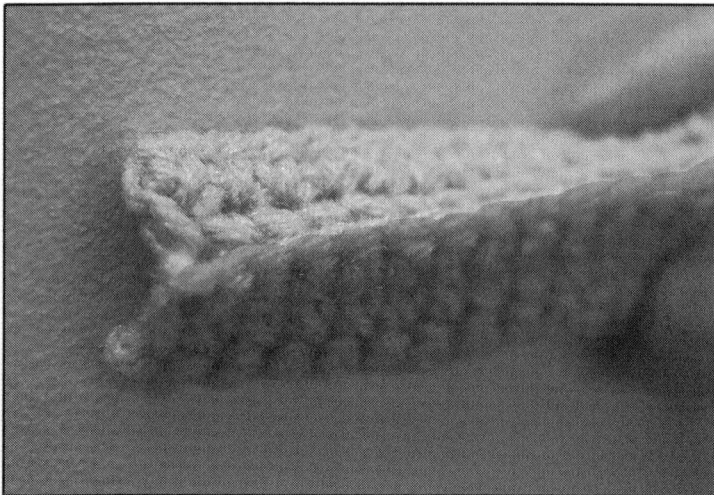

Figure 5. The line that is created when crocheting only in the back loops for one row.

# Creating Corners

In Figure 5 you can also see the corner that is created with this technique. This is helpful in creating sharp edges like those found on cubes and cylindrical shapes.

# Tips On Sewing

As much as possible, I try to avoid sewing. It is very tedious. However, there are parts of the doll that you would have to sew together. The following diagrams show the types of sewing styles used in doll making. Figure 6 shows the overcast stitch that I have used when sewing clothes for dolls. Based on the style you are going for, you can use any color yarn for the sewing thread. The type of needle you would use for this is a darning needle. The ones with the bent tip are more convenient because they can get into hard-to-reach places and pick up parts of your work better. The overcast stitch blends well with your work especially if you are using the same color yarn.

When you are making weapons for dolls or other accessories, you can layer pieces together and use the overcast stitch to sew the pieces together. Using just one layer when making a sword, for example, makes the weapon too flimsy. Layering fixes this problem. Figure 7 shows what this type of overcast stitching looks like. When you want to sew zippers onto dolls, the backstitch is typically used. This stitch is shown in Figure 8. With zippers, I use an actual sewing thread instead of yarn. Try to double up the sewing thread if it is not thick enough so that the zipper is securely attached.

Overcast stitching can also be used when attaching arms. The seams are barely visible when you do it this way. Figure 9 shows how this is done. Overcast stitching is flexible and can be used for most of the stitching you have to do when making dolls. Figure 10 shows yet another method of of connecting pieces of your work together. Instead of sewing, you can crochet pieces together. This works best with bigger items as this tends to make things bulkier.

# Tips On Sewing

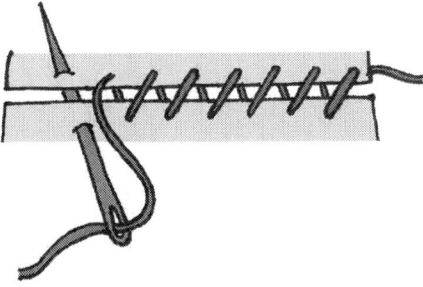

Figure 6. Overcast stitch for clothes.

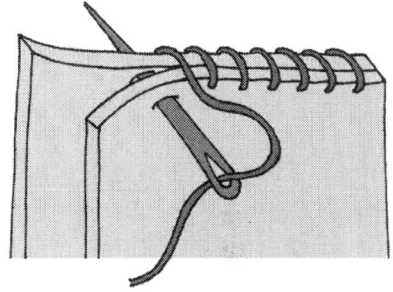

Figure 7. Overcast stitching to layer pieces together.

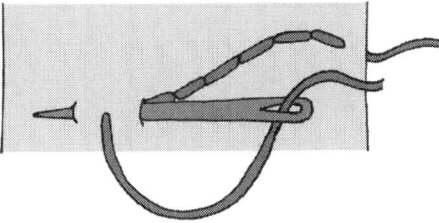

Figure 8. Backstitching.

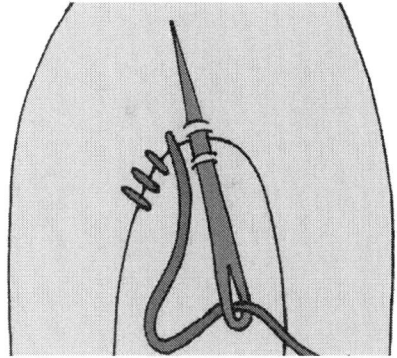

Figure 9. Attatching an arm using overcast stitching.

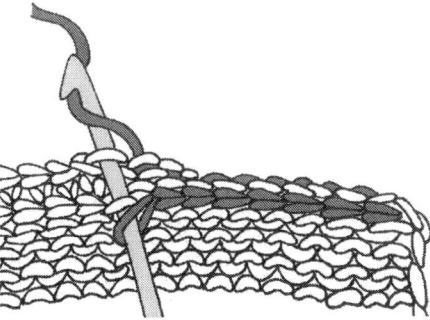

Figure 10. Crocheting two pieces together.

# Embroidering

Embroidering is useful for creating patterns on dolls. I have used this many times on dolls clothes. You can also embroider dolls faces like their eyes or mouths. There are many types of stitches but the one I typically use is the satin stitch. This is shown in Figure 11. To make this easier, it is helpful to draw the pattern you are trying to copy. Also, try to use thinner thread. However, thinner thread will take more time and effort to fill in the blank spots. Thinner thread also allows you to have greater detail and a more accurate copy of any image you choose. Just keep in mind that the more complicated the design, the bulkier it gets.

As for the needle you use, you can use any needle you are comfortable with. Since I use yarn, I use a darning needle to embroider my images. For smaller threads you would need a smaller needle. Figure 12 shows the satin stitch when creating an oval shape.

Figure 11. Satin stitch.

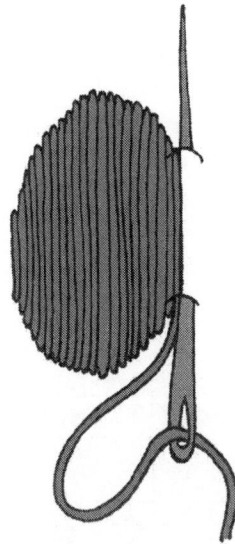

Figure 12. Making a shape with the satin stitch.

If you want to make anime-looking eyes or shapes with outlines in them, backstitching can be used for thin lines. Backstitching can also be used if you want there to be a straight edge, a sharp corner, or if your image needs more defined edges. Figure 13 is an example of a complicated anime eye that needs both satin and backstitching.

# Embroidering

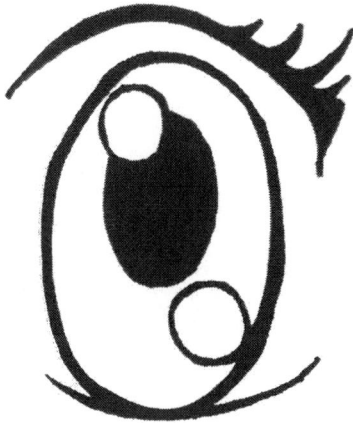

Figure 13. Anime eye.

Figure 14. Shows what a finished eye would look like. The borders of the eye are done with backstitching. The mouth is also done wth backstitching.

Figure 14. Sample eye.

# Making Fingers

Making doll hands can be tricky especially when you are making a small doll. In Appendix B, I have provided a link showing you how to create fingers. If you are having trouble creating fingers because the crochet hook is too large, try using one a size lower and see if this will make it easier to get into tough spots. I have drawn a few images to show what goes into making a doll's hand. The examples I have are for a hand with 5 fingers. Figure 15 shows an outline of what the hand should look like. The bottom part of the figure is the opening of the arm before you make the fingers. The dotted lines are the fingers.

To start the hand, divide the opening of the arm into 4 sections. Figure 16 shows how the arm is divided into sections. The number of stitches in each finger depends on how many stitches your arm has to begin with. If you ended up with 28 stitches for the arm opening, then each finger will have 7 stitches ($28 \div 4 = 7$). For the thumb, try to add 1 or 2 stitches because the thumb is typically thicker than the rest of the fingers. The thumb is outlined in Figure 16. The thumb is created first by picking up stitches on the side of the arm. The trick to creating the thumb is to pick up stitches closer to palm of the doll's hand and closer to the first finger. In this way, the doll's hand will look more natural. In Appendix B, there is a link to a video on how to pick up stitches.

Making the actual finger requires creating a slip stitch. Figure 17 shows where this is made. If you are concerned that the finger is too small, then instead of having a slip stitch, you can create a single crochet instead. This will add one more stitch to the finger so you will not have to crochet in such a tight space.

As for the height of the fingers, there is no standard height. This all depends on the size of the doll's hand. Once you have crocheted up to the desired height of the fingers, finish off and sew the gap closed.

# Making Fingers

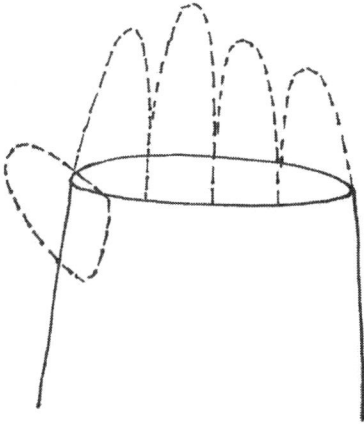

Figure 15. Outline of hand.

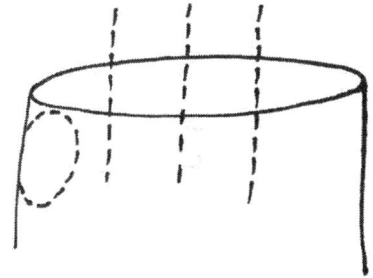

Figure 16. Dividing arm to create fingers.

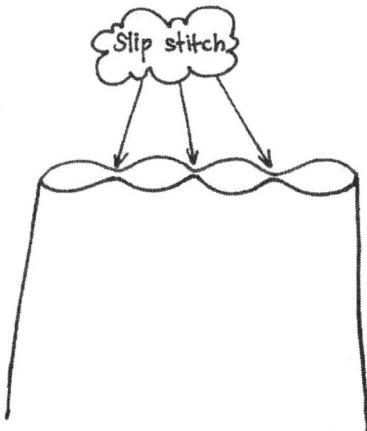

Slip stitch

Figure 17. Using slip stitches to create fingers.

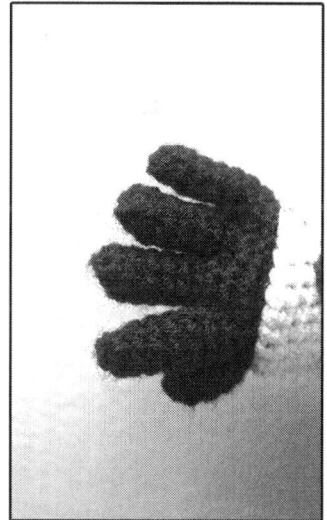

Figure 18. Sample hand.

# Attaching Arms

The trick to having even arms is to start creating both arms at the same time. After picking up stitches for one arm, cut your yarn and start the other arm (you can attach yarn later to continue this arm). This will make it easier to figure out where the second arm should be. It is easier to make even arms this way because you can see exactly where the stitches are for both arms. If you are not sure if the arms are even, try to use a ruler to help you.

This technique also works for ears and legs. Of course, this also means that you have more loose ends but at least everything will be placed where they should be.

# Clothes And Detailing

Making clothes and adding detail can be difficult sometimes and it is hard to figure out where to start. This is especially true for complicated looking garments like those worn by characters in anime shows and video games. A good place to start is to look at multiple versions of the items you want to make and see which one is the least complicated. Then, draw what you want to crochet. If the clothing is oddly shaped and cannot be made without sewing pieces together, then divide the clothing into easily manageable shapes that you can crochet. The following are examples of simple shapes you can use. These are just guides on how to start these shapes. You can modify them any way you would like. Examples of each of these shapes are shown. I will also be showing you how to create some of the details you see on dolls.

Figure 19. Sword sheath decoration made using semicircles.

In Figure 19, the decoration on the top of the sheath was made using semicircles. There are two of them. Both were folded in half and placed on opposite sides of the top part of the sheath.

# Clothes And Detailing

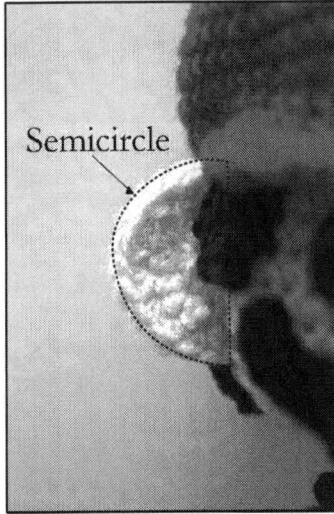

Figure 20. Semicircle used for an ear.

Semicircle:
1. Chain 2.
2. 3sc in second chain from hook. [3]
3. Chain 1. Turn work. 2sc in each st. [6]
4. Chain 1. Turn work. (1sc in first st. 2sc in next st.) 3X [9]
5. Chain 1. Turn work. (1sc in first 2 st. 2sc in next st.) 3X [12]
6. Chain 1. Turn work. (1sc in first 3 st. 2sc in next st.) 3X [15]
etcetera...

Figure 21. This hat was created using a cone shape.

# Clothes And Detailing

Cone (larger version):
1. 6sc in magic circle. [6]
2. 1sc in each st around. [6]
3. 2sc in each st around. [12]
4. 1sc in each st around. [12]
5. (1sc in first st. 2sc in next st.) 6X [18]
6. 1sc in each st around. [18]
7. (1sc in first 2 st. 2sc in next st.) 6X [24]
8. 1sc in each st around. [24]

Cone* (smaller version):
1. 4sc in magic circle. [4]
2. 1sc in each st around. [4]
3. 2sc in each st around. [8]
4. 1sc in each st around. [8]
5. (1sc in first st. 2sc in next st.) 4X [12]
6. 1sc in each st around. [12]
7. (1sc in first 2 st. 2sc in next st.) 4X [16]
8. 1sc in each st around. [16]

*As you can see, making a cone is just like making a regular circle. The only difference is that "1sc in each st around" is placed right after you increase. You can see this in steps 2, 4, 6 and 8.

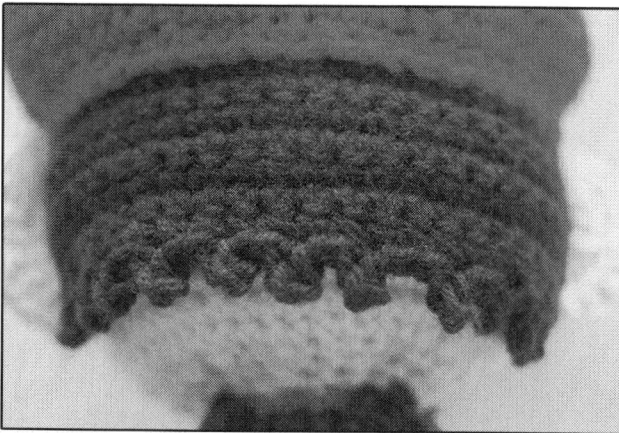

Figure 22. Hair created using picots.

# Clothes And Detailing

Picot (for hair)**:

1. Start where you want the bottom part of the hair to be.

2. Chain 1. Turn work. 1sc in first st. (Chain 5. Create sl st with first chain you created. 1sc in next 2 st.) Repeat the bracketed area until you reach the end of the row.

**This will be the detail at the bottom of the hair for those who want a change from regular strands of yarn that are typically used for hair. You would start with a rectangle shape and the picots would go at the bottom. This type of hair has a cleaner look to it.

Figure 23. Example of a mustache on a doll.

Mustache***:

1. Chain 24.

2. Starting in second chain from hook. (1sc in chain. 3 dc in next chain. 1sc in next chain. Skip two chains.) Repeat until end. You should end up with 1sc for the last chain.

***This pattern can be altered depending on the size of the doll's head.

# Clothes And Detailing

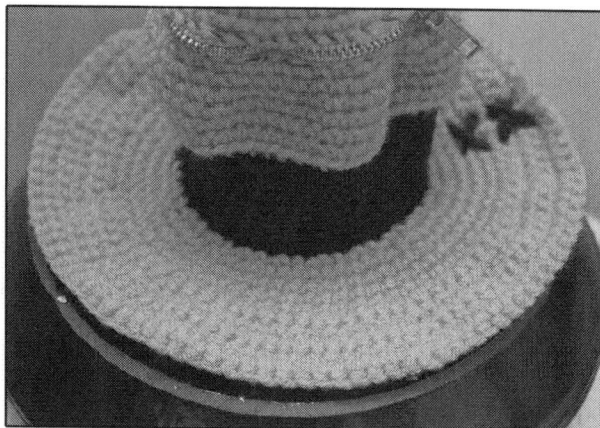

Figure 24. A mage's hat.

When you want to make a hat, you might want to fan out the bottom part so that it will form the brim. The brim is the part that projects outward and is at a 90 degree angle to the top part of the hat. Depending on the thickness of your work or your yarn, this pattern will vary. For the part of the hat that you want to fan out, you would do "2sc in each st around." The next couple of rows would then be "1sc in each st. around." Where you go from here depends on how the brim looks. You want the brim to project straight out without wrinkling. If your work starts to wrinkle or bunch up, then you have added too many stitches in that row. If the brim starts sagging downwards, then you should increase and add more stitches.

Figure 25. Using a heart on a doll. Note pink chains as a detail.

# Clothes And Detailing

Heart****:

1. Chain 4.
2. 3 triple crochets in the first chain.
3. 3 double crochets in the first chain.
4. Chain 1. 1 triple crochet in first chain. Chain 1.
5. 3 double crochets in the first chain.
6. 3 triple crochets in the first chain.
7. Chain 3.
8. Slip stitch with first chain.

****You are only working in one chain for the entire heart.

In Figure 25, you can see that I used pink chains to add the details on this particular doll. You can either embroider this or use chains. Sometimes chains are easier to use because they are thicker and you do not have to worry about filling in all the spaces.

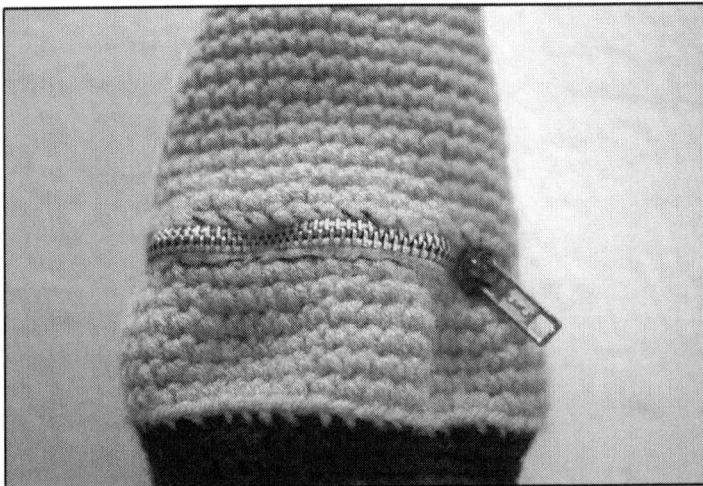

Figure 26. Zipper added on a mage's hat.

Zippers do not always have to be used in the traditional way. They can also serve as a decoration. The zipper in Figure 26 is functional. Using different type of media when making dolls is a great way of making it your own. Mixed media lets your creative juices flow and enables you to go beyond your comfort zone.

# Clothes And Detailing

Figure 27. Metal ring fasteners used on clothes.

Sometimes including a little metal to doll clothing can add a nice touch. It makes the doll look more complete. In Figure 27, the metal ring fasteners are used to add detail to the belt and the jacket.

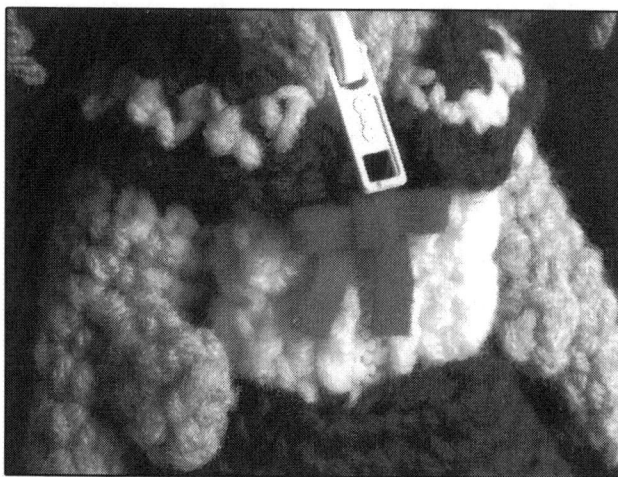

Figure 28. A bow made out of felt.

# Clothes And Detailing

Figure 29. Doll eyes made out of felt.

Felt can also be glued onto clothes. I use fabric glue because this makes the felt stay on the doll better than regular glue. I use felt when small details make it hard to make everything with yarn. Sometimes crocheting a bow or a small circle makes it too thick that it would stick out too much when it is attached. Earlier I mentioned that eyes can be embroidered. Eyes can also be made out of felt. You can glue the felt in layers to give the eye more depth.

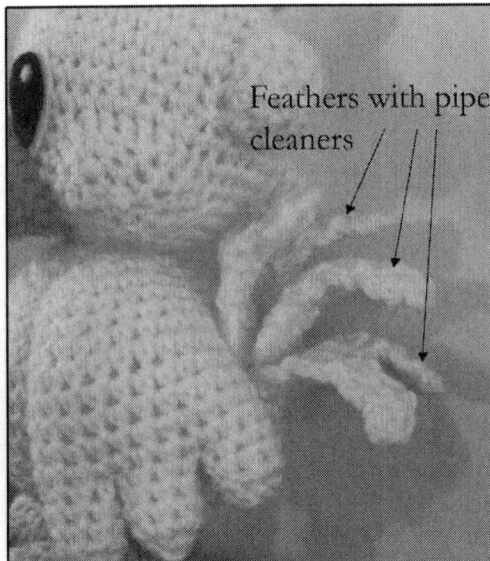

Figure 30. Pipe cleaners used for structure of feathers.

# Clothes And Detailing

There are times when you want a weapon or feathers to stay upright. Pipe cleaners are perfect for this. Try to use pipe cleaners that are the same color as the yarn you are using. If you cannot find the same color, try to hide it with yarn or at least try to match the yarn color. You might have to sew the pipe cleaners onto whatever you are making to secure them as shown in Figure 30. Aside from keeping things upright, pipe cleaners also allow you to bend whatever you put them on in any direction. In the case of the feathers in Figure 30, the feathers can be arranged in this way to make them fan out a bit.

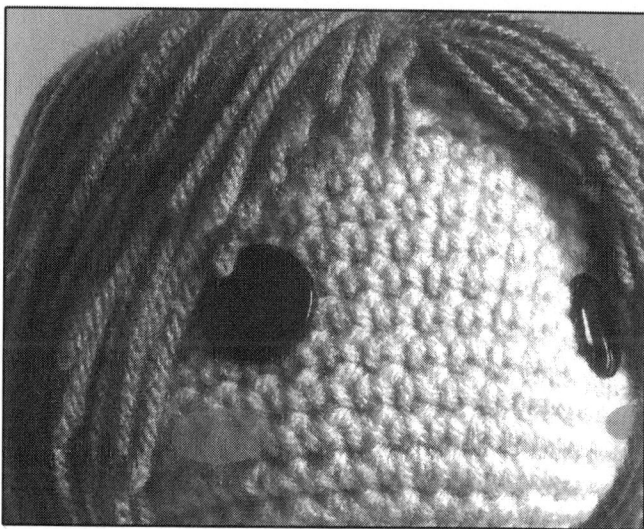

Figure 31. Cheeks stained with colored pencils.

Colored pencils are your best friend if you left out some color on your dolls, especially the cheeks. Rosy cheeks can be achieved by just brushing some color on them with pinkish or reddish colored pencils. You have to experiment a bit to get the desired look because different colors have a different effect on different types of yarn. Colored pencils take the classic rosy cheeks to another level. This allows the colors from the colored pencils to gradually blend in with color of the yarn.

# Doll Hair

Typically yarn is used for doll hair. This is a tedious process and takes a lot of yarn to do. I use the cow hitch knot for the hair. Figure 32 shows what this knot looks like. Figure 33 shows the pattern in which to place the hair. I usually start in the middle and move outwards. The dotted lines are where the hair should go. However, this is just one pattern. There are other ways in which hair can be placed on a doll's head. Less hair should be placed at the front unless the doll has bangs. Also, you do not have to have a really thick layer of hair. Just put enough so that no gaps are seen.

When cutting pieces of yarn to use as hair, it is always wise to make them a little longer that what you need because you can always shorten the hair after.

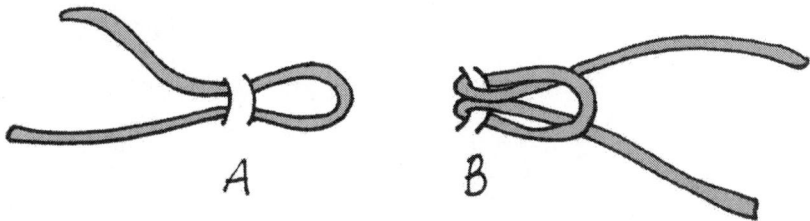

Figure 32. The cow hitch knot used for hair.

Figure 33. Pattern of hair placement.

Figure 33 shows an aerial view of the head, with the bottom of the circle being the front of the head. The front part does not need as much hair

# Doll Hair

as the rest of the head. You can even use different colored yarns for hair for added texture. Figure 34 shows you an example of a doll using two types of yellow yarn.

Figure 34. Using two types of yellow yarn for hair.

# Doll Eyes

What I do to attach doll eyes is to first locate where I want them to be. I then take 2 of my largest crochet hooks and stick them through the doll's face where the eyes should be. This should make large enough openings for the back part of a shank button or a safety eye to go through. Using a crochet hook or a ruler as a guide for even eyes can help. Make sure that the eyes are not too far from each other or too close.

Securing eyes can be difficult. The following images show one method to do this.

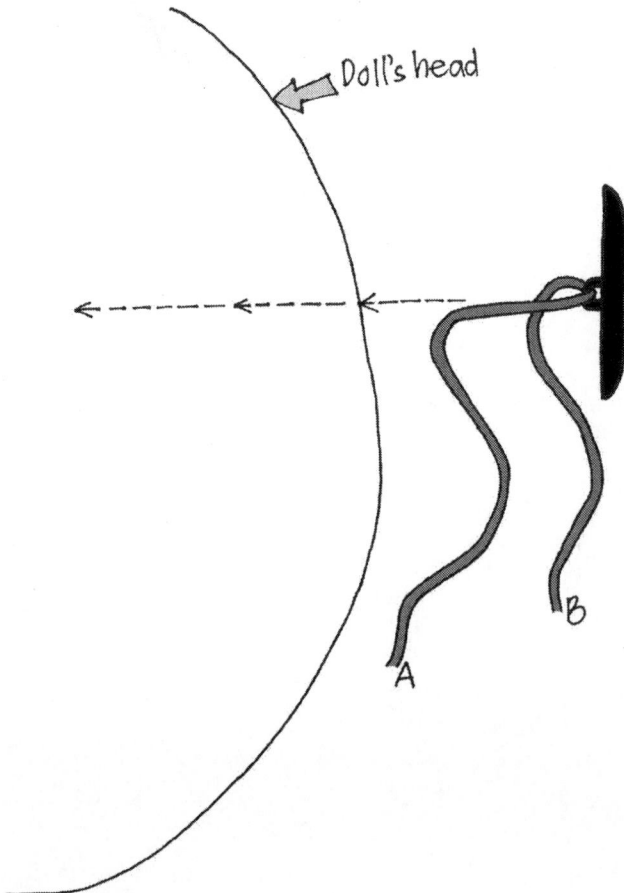

Figure 35. Adding buttons for eyes.

# Doll Eyes

First put yarn through the loop on the back of a shank button. If you are using a regular button with holes that go all the way through, try to use yarn or thread that is the same color as the button. For both types of buttons it might be difficult to put the yarn through if it is too thick. In this case try using yarn that is thinner or use thick thread instead. It may help to use a needle threader to pull yarn through if you are having trouble with this part. Once you have the yarn through the loop, make sure that the loose ends, A and B are longer than the diameter of the doll's head and somewhat equal in length with each other. Feed A and B into the doll's head as shown in Figure 35. The dotted lines show where you are to insert your darning needle. Both A and B can go through the same opening.

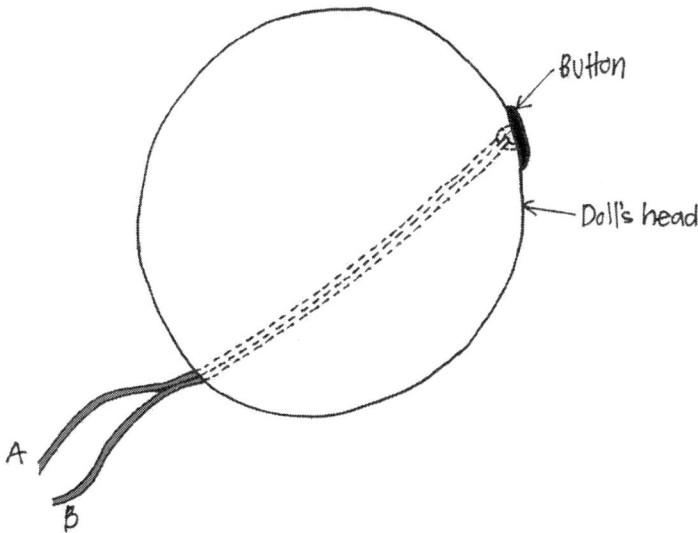

Figure 36. Feeding A and B through the doll's head.

Feed A and B all the way through to the bottom part of the doll's head. Figure 36 shows this. This part of the doll will not be seen as much so it is better to hide the knot here. Once both A and B have gone through, tug on them a little before tying a knot. This creates a slight indent where the eye is and it prevents the eye from sticking out too much. Figure 37 shows what this is suppose to look like. Keep in mind that some of the stuffing from the head may come out after pulling A and B through the head. Simply put this back in if this happens.

# Doll Eyes

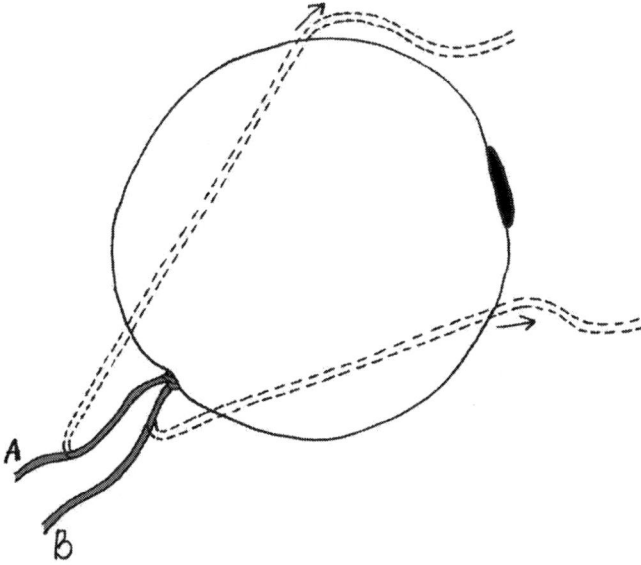

Figure 37. Hiding the loose ends.

Figure 37 also shows how to hide the loose ends after making a knot. Just feed A and B through the doll's head. Once it comes out on the other side, pull on it and cut it. The action of pulling first before cutting allows the loose end to retract back into the head, therefore hiding it.

# Loose Ends

Loose ends are dealt with in the same manner as mentioned earlier in the Doll Eyes section. Hiding loose ends can be a pain especially if you are making doll hands. I always make sure that I have an equal number of loose ends just so they can be tied together before hiding them. If you are in a situtation where you cannot do that, just make sure that some sort of knot can be made somewhere on the doll so that the loose end cannot be pulled out. Be sure to make your knots where they cannot be easily seen. At the base of the back of the head is a great spot to hide knots. Any underside surface is a good place to choose.

# Making Benjamin

# Benjamin

This is a pattern for the doll named Benjamin. He is featured on the cover of this book. He is a variation from the regular sackboy dolls I make on my YouTube channel. This pattern is an example of changing a pattern and putting your own spin to it.

What you will need:
1. Light brown yarn
2. Shiny round buttons for eyes
3. Darning needle
4. Scissors and stuffing
5. U.S. size F5/3.75 MM crochet hook

Head:
1. 6sc in magic circle.
2. 2sc in each st around. [12]
3. (1sc in first st. 2sc in next st.) 6X [18]
4. (1sc in first 2 st. 2sc in next st.) 6X [24]
5. 1sc in each st around. [24]
6. (1sc in first 3 st. 2sc in next st.) 6X [30]
7. 1sc in each st around. [30]
8. (1sc in first 4 st. 2sc in next st.) 6X [36]  1sc in 6 st
9. 1sc in each st around. For 4 rows. [36]
10. Only in the back loops. (1sc in the first 4 st. Sc2tog.) 6X [30]
11. (1sc in first 3 st. Sc2tog.) 6X [24]
12. (1sc in first 2 st. Sc2tog.) 6X [18]
13. (1sc in first st. Sc2tog.) 6X [12]
14. (Sc2tog.) 6X [6]
15. 2sc in each st around. [12]
16. (1sc in first st. 2sc in next st.) 6X [18]
17. 1sc in each st around. For 7 rows. [18]
18. Only in the back loops. (1sc in first st. Sc2tog.) 6X [12]

Legs:
1. Pick up 7 stitches at the bottom. [7]
2. 2sc in each st around. [14]
3. 1sc in each st around. For 5 rows. [14]

# Benjamin

4. Sc2tog around. Finish off and sew gap closed.

Arms:
1. Pick up 6 stitches where the arms should be. [6]
2. 2sc in each st around. [12]
3. 1sc in each st around. For 6 rows. [12]
4. Create 2 fingers and a thumb. 6 st for each finger and thumb.

Now that you have finished the basic doll you can change the colors however you would like.

# Appendices

# Appendix A
## Terms And Abbreviations

There are other terms used in crochet patterns but these are the most commonly used when you are making dolls. I use these often when making my patterns.

Back loop - loop away from you
ch - chain
dc - double crochet
FO - finish off
Front loop - loop closest to you
sc - single crochet
st - stitch
sc2tog - single crochet 2 together
tog - together

Below are other terms you might see in other patterns or might want to use in yours.

dec - decrease
inc - increase
patt - pattern
rep - repeat
rnd - round
RS - right side
sl st - slip stitch
WS - wrong side
yo - yarn over

Here is a conversion for US/UK terms.

single crochet - double crochet
half double crochet - half treble
double crochet - treble
triple crochet - double treble
skip - miss

# Appendix B
GoldenJellyBean Links

1. Regular circle: http://www.youtube.com/watch?v=lzlIGtGtPvY

2. Magic circle: http://www.youtube.com/watch?v=M5IGo9IeU58

3. Picking up  stitches: http://www.youtube.com/watch?v=yKCFP wbg7jM

4. Creating fingers: http://www.youtube.com/watch?v=Sm9xuh2Onh8

# Appendix C
## GJB Social Pages And Websites

YouTube:

http://www.youtube.com/user/GoldenJellyBean

http://www.youtube.com/user/FullMetalPiglet

Website/Blog:

http://goldenjellybean.com

Pattern Shops:

https://www.etsy.com/shop/GJBCrochet

http://www.ravelry.com/stores/gjbcrochet

http://goldenjellybean.com/pattern-shop/

Facebook:

https://www.facebook.com/Goldenjellybean

https://www.facebook.com/GeekOutWithGjb

Twitter:

https://twitter.com/Goldenjellybean

deviantArt:

http://goldenjellybean.deviantart.com

Printed in Great Britain
by Amazon.co.uk, Ltd.,
Marston Gate.